THE
ELOQUENCE
OF
LIVING

THE
ELOQUENCE
OF
LIVING

Meeting Life with Freshness,
Fearlessness, and Compassion

VIMALA THAKAR

NEW WORLD LIBRARY · SAN RAFAEL, CALIFORNIA

© 1989 Vimala Programs California

Published by New World Library
58 Paul Drive
San Rafael, California

Cover design & Text illustration: Charles Powell
Text design: Nancy Benedict
Typography: Walker Graphics

First printing, October, 1989
ISBN 0-931432-61-8
10   9   8   7   6   5   4   3   2   1

CONTENTS

FREEDOM 1

RELATEDNESS 15

RELIGIOUS INQUIRY 31

OBSERVATION 49

INNER ORDER 65

AWARENESS 75

SILENCE 83

MEDITATION 101

PREFACE

Vimala Thakar is passionately in love with living. She meets the challenges of a complex society in a simple, elegant, perceptive way. She speaks as a lifelong inquirer into truth, into freedom, and into the essence of religion. If one can live in a state of sustained inquiry, she says, a new energy with a new mode of behavior will come into play.

Although educated as a philosopher, studying both eastern and western philosophy, she has been since youth actively expressing her approach to living in programs of social action such as the Vinoba Bhave Land Gift Movement, and, currently, the Jeevan Yoga Foundation work of promoting village self-sufficiency.

In these programs, Vimala has traveled thousands of miles through India, moving from village to village, talking with people about local problems and about projects that will encourage more active involvement in the democratic process. Her work blends the spiritual and social in a total approach to the challenges of living.

She speaks not of escaping from society, but of meeting society, the challenges of daily living, with freshness, fearlessness, and compassion.

THE GIFT

I have come to sing
The song of life
I know not how to teach.

I have come to love
The diversity of life
I know not how to preach.

I have come to live
A sane healthy life
I know not how to lead.

My heart is a lotus.
These words are petals.
This is my gift to you.

FREEDOM

There is something in each human heart that whispers:

"You are free.

"You are not born to live in bondage, in shackles of the past; you are not born to oscillate between attachments and detachments.

"You are born to live in love."

2

FREEDOM

Growth into the freedom of peace and silence is not the privilege of a chosen few.

It's the natural state of being for everyone.

We don't have to create freedom; it is there as the substance of reality.

We have only to let the false drop noiselessly.

We shrink back from freedom because in freedom there is no belonging, except to all.

FREEDOM

Unless we understand the content of our whole being, freedom cannot be.

Freedom is not a speculative, romantic game of imagining something which is not.

It is simply comprehension of what is.

4

FREEDOM

Our lives can be charged with freedom, the bliss of peace and the dynamism of joy, or they can become dark and heavy with our indifference, our careless, fleeting moods.

The choice is ours.

If we have lost respect for life, lost sensitivity of living, we cannot be free.

FREEDOM

Can it be that we have not discovered the essence of living?

Can it be that we are committed only to earning a livelihood, to following the patterns of a society intoxicated with the power of science and technology, and have created a world where natural living is no more?

FREEDOM

We have made space and time shrink before us, through science and technology, and we have reduced the world to a small human family.

We have done all this, and yet we are not at peace with ourselves.

Collectively how sad we are.

We spend all our lives acquiring, and yet we depart from the world empty-handed and empty-hearted, not having the satisfaction of having lived in love, in communion with life, in the bliss of freedom.

7

FREEDOM

As human beings we are not mature.

We have not learned how to live in peace with ourselves, in friendship with others, in communion with all of life.

We have learned how to exploit life, but not how to gently, tenderly love life.

8

FREEDOM

When one feels surrounded by darkness, one can either lapse into feelings of helplessness and depression, spreading antisocial currents of frustration, bitterness, and cynicism, or one can gather the small tender lamp of one's intelligence and understanding and walk in the light of that.

If each person sees that his or her corner is illuminated, there is nothing that remains a global problem.

FREEDOM

We must create a society in which a person does not have to betray inner sensitivity, inner essence.

Each of us needs opportunities to unfold the essence of being.

Then the sensitivity becomes a foundation of strength, of peace, of joy.

FREEDOM

If truth and love, mutual respect and concern, affection and friendship have any value in life, then the social, economic, and political structures will have to be changed and adjusted to these, not our inner life adjusted to the outer structures.

11

FREEDOM

When we feel exhausted by the insanity, disorder, and imbalance around us and are ready to bring about an inner change, we might keep in mind that learning a technique or a method to artificially stimulate experiences brings only partial change.

The challenge is not to alter partially the status of physical or mental life; the challenge is total growth into another dynamic of relationship and into another dimension of consciousness.

FREEDOM

Living is something which is done in totality.
A flower which is blossoming unfolds every petal.
The beauty and the scent which were hidden in the
bud come out completely.
A fruit when it ripens, grows ripe in its totality.
But we human beings grow partially, in fragments.

We refine and cultivate the intellect, body, physical
surroundings, and the psychological structures as
fragments, unaware that total living unfolds a dimension
of consciousness which we have not yet explored. If we
have the urge to live fully, totally, as marvelous, complete,
mature expressions of humanity, we must meet life
sensitively, alertly with each day that dawns.

13

FREEDOM

When any one of us says: "I will live tomorrow," he or she is indulging in a dangerous fantasy about living.

The life that the dawn brings us is the only life we have.

Life is in the here and now, not in the there and afterwards.

The day, with all the travail and joy that it brings to our doorstep, is the expression of eternal life.

Either we meet it, we live it—or we miss it.

RELATEDNESS

What we do in our so-called daily living is repeat patterns of behavior which we have cultivated, acquired, and inherited. Physically, mentally, verbally, we indulge in mechanistic movement throughout the day. In this repetitive substitute for living, there is no joy, no charm, no grace.

Is it possible to take a fresh look at daily living, innocently like a child?

RELATEDNESS

There is only overwhelming boredom with repeating day after day, year after year, lifeless, joyless activities.

Worn out by these repetitive, mechanistic patterns of living, tired of feeling isolated from fellow human beings, we long for a richer, more meaningful life.

Is it possible to notice as for the first time the intricate, charming world waiting to commune with us?

RELATEDNESS

You stand at the seashore perhaps knee-deep in water observing the skies, the wide horizons, the openness.

You listen to the birds; they are singing for their own joy.

You listen and the sounds do something to you.

It's a happening.

The only requirement is to be there.

In the simplicity of your being, communion takes place.

You are not seeking, but something is bestowed on you, something touches you at all levels.

RELATEDNESS

Life is poetry.
It is music.
The sound vibrations flowing among all that exists
have a music of their own, untouched by man.

The earth has a language of its own; bounty, nectar,
colors, textures, and intricate rhythms are the language of
Mother Earth.

When you visit golden fields, the crops ripe but not
yet harvested, when you talk to the dancing rice or wheat
fields, then you understand the language of Mother Earth.

RELATEDNESS

Life speaks eloquently within and around you.
If you are greatly sensitive and alert, you can receive
its communications, understand and respond to its elegant
expressions, its thrilling songs.

RELATEDNESS

Learning how to commune with life requires humility.

When you are caught up in the arrogance of knowing or are repeating mechanically predetermined patterns, humility and learning cannot happen.

On a beautiful morning you walk in the woods.

You are alone with the woods, the light and the shadow, the shades of green leaves freshly bathed with rain, sun rays dancing on the branches through the leaves to the ground.

You did not go there to acquire something.

You went there to be with the trees, with other beings.

To be, not to obtain, not to acquire.

RELATEDNESS

When you have the humility to be with people in the simplicity of what you are, not pretending to be what you are not, not trying to hide what you are, then communion takes place. You understand the other person more deeply than all knowledge could make possible.

You notice that a new tenderness of affection begins to blossom.

RELATEDNESS

Humility, the urge to learn and to discover, the quiet communion of being without the motive of acquiring, permits the growth of understanding.

Understanding is like a mountain stream that breaks through the rocks and dances, making its own way.

When understanding dawns, it finds its own way through your life, changing attitudes, approaches, habit patterns.

It penetrates as gentle water penetrates rock.
As the mountain streams have a tremendous force, understanding also has an irresistible force.

RELATEDNESS

Your total being is involved in the event of understanding.

You are aware of being organically related to the whole universe at every moment.

Though life's many aspects and infinite variety of forms give an appearance of duality, understanding brings awareness of the undercurrent of unity.

RELATEDNESS

We live in duality and know unity only as a theory. We are all too familiar with the endless pressures of feeling apart, isolated, and the tiresome worries of being in competition with our fellow beings, but we don't know the marvelous ease of living, the soft rhythms, when the myth of separation dissolves.

RELATEDNESS

Most of our actions are expressions of the fragmentation and not the unity of life.

We live with inner fragmentation, incompatible sets of values struggling with each other, ambitions and desires that are not correlated with the total life, compulsions that pull us in ten directions in ten hours.

We feel the emotional chaos, it tires us, and at the end of the day we are worn out, irritable.

We go on fragmenting ourselves, dividing ourselves, tearing ourselves to pieces, but life remains whole.

All the philosophies, psychologies and sciences, all the imaginary divisions and compartments that we have arranged for the convenience of collective living cannot fragment the wholeness of life.

RELATEDNESS

Have you noticed that all the beings who share the earth are interrelated?

Have you looked at the companions with whom we live—the fellow oceans and rivers?

When we are busy with our city life, we have little opportunity to feel their presence.

We hardly have an opportunity to be in dialogue with the vast skies and their colors, with the daylight and the night, to feel the presence of the earth beneath our feet, and to get thrilled by the solidity, the pull of gravity, the tenderness, the hardness of the earth.

RELATEDNESS

When sensitivity to the oneness of life dawns, there is openness and humility, there is communion with all the manifestations of life, there is relaxation of competition and conflict, there is an easy grace to relationships.

With this sensitivity, whom can you hate?
Whom can you exploit?
Whom can you kill?

RELATEDNESS

The awareness of unity in relationships is love.
It is vulnerability.
Love is its own protection.
Truth is its own security.
All other securities created by man's mind are hollow.

RELATEDNESS

Nothing in life is trivial.
Life is whole wherever and whenever we touch it, and one moment or event is not less sacred than another.

RELIGIOUS INQUIRY

Religion is a way of living in which the totality, the beautiful wealth inside, is involved every moment in every relationship.

The manipulation of sound in speech, the mysterious process of breathing, the sense organs of looking, listening, touching are involved. You see the interrelatedness of all the energies of the cosmos in your own body, the relationships among the earth, the water, the sky.

RELIGIOUS INQUIRY

Everything can be watched in the individual because the individual is a miniature cosmos—all the energies that are operating in the infinite space of the cosmos are operating here.

To be religious is to live in communion with life in all its aspects of unity and diversity, peace and movement, silence and speech, birth and death.

Life is a tremendous mystery, a constant interplay of energy, a miracle.

RELIGIOUS INQUIRY

The essence of religion is the personal discovery of the meaning of life, the truth of life.

Religion is related to the unconditional, total freedom that truth confers on us.

It is a revolution of the whole way of living. Religion moves us from the superficial layers of existence and encourages us to go deeper to the roots of life.

It is an inward journey to the depths of our being.

RELIGIOUS INQUIRY

A religious inquiry requires the humility to learn at every step.

Learning is living.

One who learns lives fully and never becomes stale till the last breath of life.

The fragrance of freshness is always with this attitude of learning.

RELIGIOUS INQUIRY

If I want to discover the truth of life, the meaning of life, I will have to begin learning and discovering for myself without the authority of another person.

If I accept the authority of a person, dogma, or ideology, I lose freedom at the very first step of the inner voyage.

If I choose from various patterns of authority, select one and try to approximate my life to that, I am bargaining with the search for freedom.

RELIGIOUS INQUIRY

Understanding that acceptance of authority is not the way to freedom, let me begin with humility as an explorer, beginning with my own life to find out what is truth.

RELIGIOUS INQUIRY

Let me begin by saying,
"I do not know what God is, what reality is, what death is, what freedom is.

"Let me find out."

In that state of humility, in that openness to learning, I become a disciple—not to an authority, but to life, to universal, cosmic life which is the ancient master and teacher.

Nothing teaches as life does, by throwing up challenges ever fresh and ever new.

Every dawn brings a new challenge to the doorstep.

Life is willing to teach those who are willing to learn for themselves.

RELIGIOUS INQUIRY

If we can be disciples of our own understanding, we shall see that life changes, growth takes place.

If we can listen to the inner understanding fearlessly, innocently, then education takes place.

Have you noticed how defensive and apologetic we are before our own intelligence?

The intelligence points out when we indulge in falsehoods, in laziness, when we postpone actions and decisions, but we plead our case, we ignore, defend, and betray our own understanding.

RELIGIOUS INQUIRY

If we betray our own understanding, who on earth is going to save us?

If we have the cheek to deceive ourselves, who is going to lift us out of this vicious game of self-deception?

RELIGIOUS INQUIRY

Education takes place when we have the humility to listen to the voice of understanding that speaks in our hearts and to act on that understanding instantaneously, not allowing it to fade into dead memories, losing all dynamic force, all vitality for transforming our lives.

Life is fulfilled by the act of perception, understanding, and living the understanding.

RELIGIOUS INQUIRY

Understanding has a penetrating clarity.
It has no heaviness, indistinctness.
It is a clear flame, a smokeless flame that suddenly
burns in the heart.
It leaves no choice for selection, no space to bargain
for the favorable consequences or to try to dodge
unfavorable ones.

RELIGIOUS INQUIRY

Understanding may reveal the limitations of long-cherished traditions and ideologies.

Suddenly fear grips you.

"If I act on my understanding, what will my friends say?

"What will my family do?

"What will happen to me?"

The desire for security seeks to maintain the status quo, but the inner aspiration for discovery of truth requires a person to be open, vulnerable.

You may not see the incompatibility of the two. You may try to take a little part of your understanding and act on it today and a little more tomorrow and act on that.

But understanding is not like a loaf of bread which you can take a slice at a time, one slice today and another tomorrow. Understanding comes as a vibrant whole, challenging the total being to live fearlessly, tenderly, openly.

RELIGIOUS INQUIRY

Religious inquiry involves willingness to court failure.

If we are too much concerned with doing the correct thing and are afraid of making mistakes, then fear creates inhibitions and prevents the openness necessary for learning.

Sometimes we'll make mistakes, slip and fall, but as children learning to walk, we pick ourselves up and go on joyously, carrying no grudge about the pains of the fall.

The moment that fear disappears, the fear of what is acceptable, of what others will think, understanding unfolds and reveals what is true, what is holy.

RELIGIOUS INQUIRY

If understanding points out what is true, simultaneously it points out what is false.

When I have understood the false as the false, and if there is no attachment to the false, the false drops away as the winter leaves fall from a tree without hurting the tree.

The false, the untruth gathered in the psyche with the dust of years, drops away when the true is revealed.

RELIGIOUS INQUIRY

As human beings we have tremendous potential for changing, growing, transforming.
We share divinity with the cosmos around us.
We are potentially divine.

RELIGIOUS INQUIRY

When there is no fear of living and no fear of dying, we can realize our potential for growth.

We would like the river of life to move as the calm waters of a protected canal; we don't want the river to thrust us into the mainstream with rapids and white water, exposed, vulnerable.

But vulnerability has a beauty, a significance.

It's only when we're willing to be vulnerable, unprotected by fixed ideas, traditions, and habitual ways, that the adventure of self-discovery, the inward voyage can begin.

OBSERVATION

Growth, transformation begins with a firsthand investigation of your own mind. It begins with being aware of what you are doing and why you are doing it.

You may read a hundred books, but unless you look at the movement of mind from moment to moment, you will never understand what the mind is.

The state of being aware of what you are doing and why you are doing it is the foundation of inner peace.

OBSERVATION

Whenever you use your mind, you have to educate yourself to be there totally, not absentmindedly, half-heartedly, but pouring your whole being into it.

To be attentive is to be sensitive.

The mind is alert, sensitive, attentive only in the absence of habit.

When you go through an event absentmindedly, passively, out of habit, you are not there.

The wholeness of your being has missed the opportunity for living.

Habit moves, not you.

Mechanical repetition creates an illusion of living, but there is neither encounter with life nor growth.

OBSERVATION

Inattention has become a way of living.
It is our chief psychological luxury.
To be fully present, to be alert and sensitive is something we typically choose not to do.
Unless attentiveness pervades every aspect of our living, every encounter with another, there is no possibility for communion to take place.

OBSERVATION

Where does the hard work of meeting each day, each relationship attentively begin?

It begins with observation, with seeing your life as it actually is.

Observing the flowers and the trees is easy.

Observing the stream of thoughts while sitting quietly by yourself is not difficult.

But to observe the momentum of mind while you are living and working requires energy, tremendous sensitivity, and alertness.

OBSERVATION

You begin observing the interplay of emotions in your daily living.

You observe that you are jealous.

You see a person richer than you and you feel jealous, not because he or she is rich, but because you feel poor; you see a person more beautiful than you, and your jealousy rises up.

Your feeling has little to do with the other person.

It emerges from discontent with the reality of your own life.

Jealousy is not a feeling directed towards others; it is a feeling directed against yourself.

The feeling arises when you are not reconciled to the fact of what you are.

OBSERVATION

To be free of jealousy does not require codes of conduct or special discipline.

It requires only that you see that jealousy or envy is the result of your dissatisfaction with yourself; it requires that you face what you are.

Your observation becomes a searchlight on the reality of your life.

When you have seen how the movement of the ego creates jealousy and envy, you have seen all the mischief of the ego and you have invited freedom to move into your life.

OBSERVATION

You observe anger; you see all the ugliness that emotions such as anger create biologically and psychologically.

The body generates heat, blood rushes to the head, circulates faster, the breathing is shaky, jerky.

The whole nervous system is tense.

You may not face the fact of anger and go to the root of it. You may go only to the superficial cause, "The other person is difficult and irritating," or to the remote cause, "My mother and father were temperamental; I have inherited the tendency."

You try to console yourself by justifying the anger.

OBSERVATION

Through observation you see that anger is a movement of the ego which expects the whole world to behave according to its idiosyncracies.

When its expectations are thwarted, the ego puts out its fangs like a serpent ready to attack, creating new mischief, and so the cycle goes on.

If you can go to the root of anger through observation, you can see the movement of the ego, and emotional disturbances—anger, jealousy, fear, violence—no longer hold you in their tenacious grip.

OBSERVATION

We see that we are afraid and being afraid we are helpless.

We're afraid of the simple facts of our lives, we're afraid of the unpredictable challenges of living, and we're afraid of dying.

We attempt to run away from living and dying, but what we think are safe harbors are illusions and they offer no protection. We try to escape, to cleverly dodge living, but life is ever there offering its challenges, and death—the fact of death—never disappears. We observe that running away solves nothing. It creates more fear, more desperate grasping for security, and more dark clouds of depression.

When we see that escape is impossible, we stand where we are and meet what comes, whatever the consequences. We find that in meeting life we are no longer helpless. We have vitality, joy for the whole business of living.

OBSERVATION

We observe our relationships, and often see that they are occasions for torment.

We judge each other even before we have communed with one another.

The mind is busy reacting, evaluating, comparing.

Before another person has even spoken, the likes and dislikes come up—the clothes, the way of talking and walking, the features.

Before we listen to a word spoken, we have judged according to norms and criteria.

And when the other person speaks, the pitch, volume, tone, expression, and message have created emotional or intellectual reactions.

We are trying to measure human beings with norms or criteria that our minds have prepared yesterday or the thousands of yesterdays of the whole human race.

OBSERVATION

To *meet* another human being is to be attentive, open, vulnerable.

It requires being with others in the simplicity of what you are, dropping all manmade pretenses and disguises.

When you meet another in the simplicity of being, observing rather than reacting, understanding and communion will be there.

OBSERVATION

In the beginning observation may not be easy; suddenly likes and dislikes arise, judgments come, deep-rooted habits assert themselves.

Before you know it, the state of observation lapses into a state of interpretation, evaluation, judgment.

But if you want to learn how to observe, avoid struggling with the lapses, simply become aware of them.

Be aware that you are not observing and observe again.

If you do not condemn yourself, do not run away, if you can be satisfied with simple awareness of inattention, nonobservation, then your sensitivity will grow and the duration of your observation will gradually increase.

OBSERVATION

In the state of observation, the past has no role to play; the past prevents taking a fresh look for it constantly reminds one of old viewpoints.

The movement of the past, being of no relevance, goes into abeyance in the state of observation.

Whatever the mind or the situation exposes to your attention, you observe.

The faculties of the analyzer, the interpreter are suspended.

Only attention burns bright.

OBSERVATION

You see pain and you see tears.

You see that tears are as much a part of life as smiles.

You live through the tears, but you do not carry the tears from today to tomorrow, the heaviness of one day to the next.

You live through whatever happens, thoroughly, fully, and then you are finished with it.

Bringing an end to the yesterdays makes possible freshness and alertness for the new challenges life brings to your door.

INNER ORDER

When the state of observation is sustained, it changes the quality of your biological structure.

The nerves are steady, the chemical system has an equilibrium, and there is relaxation, equipoise.

You live in the clarity of knowing who you are.

INNER ORDER

A relaxed state leads to humility which is the alchemy of life.

Humility transforms so many things in a human being.

Humility makes you tender, not soft and weak, but tender, pliable.

The rejuvenation that takes place through humility is something worth discovering for yourself.

INNER ORDER

When we discover humility, relationships are no longer ordeals.

We're able to meet and relate to the totality of another person, who is ever-changing.

We meet another with a fresh glance and the innocence of newness.

We have the alertness to meet life in all its rhythms, in all its unpredictability, ever new, ever mysterious.

INNER ORDER

When innocence emerges in relationship, there is opportunity for love.

You may not be acquainted with the dimension of love.

You may be busy all the time yielding to attractions or riding over the arrogance of detachments.

You may be so busy with attachment and detachment on the superficial level that you have no time to go to the depth of real love.

Attractions or repulsions never allow you to go to the depth of love.

You float on the surface; you are pulled this way or pushed that way and never arrive at love.

INNER ORDER

You may know the pains of possessing and dependency, reducing persons to objects, but this is not love.

Love doesn't attempt to bind, ensnare, capture.
It is light, free of the burden of attachments.

Love asks nothing, is fulfilled in itself.
When love is there, nothing remains to be done.

INNER ORDER

Religious inquiry into the meaning of life, into living beautifully, aesthetically, sanely begins with observation.

When observation is sustained you are attentive to all the details of living, learning to go through these details elegantly.

If you learn to take care of the details of life sensitively, joyfully, the big issues take care of themselves.

When you learn to prepare the meals, clean the house, exercise the body with joy, you will have a firm grasp on the master key to inner happiness.

INNER ORDER

Unless you put the house of your life—the physical and verbal structures—in order, the urge for exploration of that which is beyond time and space will remain only a wish in the mind.

If there is disorder in the simple things of life like diet, sleep, exercise, and breathing, trying to build a structure of exploration will be like building a house in the sand. To bring order to casual living, it is not necessary to take vows: "I must eat this; I must not eat that."

That is not the way of self-education.

You must discover for yourself what the body needs for health and what the mind needs for sanity.

You need to learn how to bring elegant simplicity, cleanliness, and order to the inner home.

INNER ORDER

You will have to equip the physical and mental structures for religious exploration.

If your nerves are weak and you become upset with the slightest experience, you won't have the balance, the strength necessary.

If somebody says something that offends you and your mind carries a grudge, spoiling the whole day, shattering inner peace, then obviously the mental and physical structures are not ready for a new dimension of life, a new dimension of consciousness.

INNER ORDER

Living in inner orderliness helps the physical and mental structures become more sensitive.

In the midst of noise, you live a quiet life.

In the midst of the brutality of comparison, competition, aggression, you live in a simple, noncomparative, nonaggressive way so that there are minimal psychological disturbances.

Sanity emerges in your life, equanimity and balance become the qualities of daily living.

AWARENESS

Observation and inner order make possible the unfolding of awareness.

Awareness is all-inclusive attention.

You are aware of the whole of life, aware of birth and death as two points on a line.

When you see birth as the beginning of death and death as the beginning of birth, when you see this cycle, your fears vanish.

The two points lose the tension of opposites and become one cyclical rhythm, the rhythm of life.

AWARENESS

Just imagine what life would be like if there were birth and no death.

Where would be the charm in living if there were only darkness or only light?

The totality embraces birth and death, light and dark, pleasure and pain.

When you live in the awareness of the totality, you are not exclusively attracted to beauty and pleasure. You see the beauty and the ugliness, the pleasure and pain as organic parts of life.

The awareness of the indivisible wholeness of life never leaves you.

It becomes a normal dimension of the psyche.

Even the thoughts are bathed in the holy waters of awareness.

AWARENESS

We don't know dying.

To die easily and gracefully without the inhibition of fear is a holy event, as holy as the event of birth.

But we are so caught up in fear of death; the word "death" frightens us, and even the idea makes us shiver.

When we see the wholeness of being born, living, and dying, there is a joy in living and a grace in dying.

AWARENESS

When you live in awareness, you go through every experience, every relationship so completely that you never need to look back; the burden of dark memory is never carried to the next moment.

This simple, innocent unwinding and expressing of your being is a sacred thing.

In awareness you live so that the very act of living leaves behind the perfume of dying.

It is only in awareness that living creatively is possible.

AWARENESS

Awareness melts the apparent divisions between living and dying, silence and sound, light and dark.

One sees life as a whole, unfragmented, just as one sees the water of an ocean undivided though thousands of people have made thousands of designs on its surface.

The indivisibility, the unfragmentable totality is the beauty of life.

AWARENESS

Awareness of the wholeness of life moves a person easily and gracefully to explore dimensions of consciousness, energy beyond the superficial.

When we explore life's wholeness, untouched by words, when we live in its freshness, its limitlessness, we see for ourselves the sacred, the holy, without which life has no meaning.

AWARENESS

As fish are born of water, live and move in water, we are born of energy, live and move in energy.

Part of this energy is conditioned, part is unconditioned.

We know well the conditioned energy of habits, memories, the movement of the past.

This conditioned energy induces pleasure but never awakens joy, enables us to experience but never gives us the bliss of total relaxation, helps us to develop defenses, but never permits the flowering of innocence.

We do not know the dimension of unconditional relaxation which permits deep understanding of living to take place.

SILENCE

If we want to understand life, to know of death, peace, love, we have to step away, go beyond the conditioned realm of mental movements and dive into silence, into complete relaxation of the conditioned mental movement.

SILENCE

Leaving the shore of word and sound, we plunge into the sea of silence, into space uncluttered by thought, and there we are nourished.

We know nothing of silence; it is an uncharted sea.

We don't know how deep it is, but we know that before we can learn to swim in the sea, we must plunge into it.

SILENCE

When movement, activity, is not necessary, relax into silence.

It is like exhaling and inhaling.

The mental movement is like exhalation, and the relaxation is like inhalation.

So throughout the day there is a rhythm of working, relaxing, like exhaling, inhaling.

They are not separate from each other.

When work, activity, relationships come to an end, you relax into silence as one movement, not two points of duality having a tension between them.

Relationships and solitude, speech and silence, movement and peace, though they have the superficial appearance of duality, are blended in the oneness of living.

SILENCE

Going beyond the brain, transcending its dimensions, is not turning your back on the content of culture.

It is not running away or announcing:

"All that is worthless for it is not the absolute reality."

Going beyond the brain, you enter into elegant simplicity, but the elegance of simplicity requires a very mature being.

You require maturity to understand the complex whole of life and live that complexity in a simple way.

SILENCE

Relaxation is a tremendous event.

In the relaxation of the mind, when thoughts do not move and emotions do not stir, when neurologically and chemically there is absolute equilibrium, the intelligence, the unconditioned energy begins to operate.

This nonpersonal, unconditioned intelligence is the nature of life, the whole of it, undefined and indescribable.

This intelligence, like beauty, love, sorrow or joy, which are its expressions, cannot be captured in shapes and forms, in definitions and descriptions.

All this is why life is worth living.

SILENCE

If I have not finished with the conditioned mind, if I still feel obsessed with the pleasure and pain that the mind can give, there will be resistance to immersion in the realm of silence.

So if I am not finished with the pleasure and pain that thoughts and emotions can give, let me go through them with my whole attention, and some day that total attention will reveal the repetitive, mechanistic nature of the conditioned mind.

Pleasure and pain will open and enter into a dialogue with me and show me their frontiers.

SILENCE

We keep ourselves busy, surrounded by people all the time, forgetting that solitude is as much a substance of life as relationship.

Whenever life offers an opportunity to be alone, we feel lonely because there is fear of being with the unfamiliar dimensions of living within each of us.

In silence, when the psyche is denuded of all identification, all sense of belonging, the fear of loneliness disappears.

We can return to relationships, to being with others, without clinging to them, depending on them.

We can enjoy being with people and being alone.

We can be joyous about living without being frightened about death.

SILENCE

You can sit without making a sound for ten hours a day and not be in silence.

If you seek to experience silence, you will never be free of the tension, the drive of motive.

If you sit in silence, waiting to experience something, expecting something special to happen, like what has happened to others, there is no relaxation.

Accepting the authority of another's experience in any way, hoping to experience what others have experienced, precludes the total relaxation that is silence.

SILENCE

Solitude, silence, and freedom are the great nourishers of life.

We think we are nourishing ourselves with words, ideas, and thoughts, but though these things are the content of consciousness, they are not the substance of reality.

SILENCE

In silence there is freedom.

In innocence there is love and in humility there is intelligence.

Silence brings you directly, intimately into communion with life as it is.

Being with the solitude of silence, being with the limitless, nameless, measureless reality creates a new balance; it refreshes the worn-out mind and washes the psyche clean of fears.

SILENCE

Stillness of the mind is one thing and silence, the total relaxation of conscious and unconscious mind into nonaction, is another.

You can take drugs to make the mind still.

You can chant to make the mind still.

You can create stillness of the mind artificially, systematically by subtle violence against the brain, but when you emerge from this stillness, the quality of the mind, the quality of living has not changed.

SILENCE

Silence is not artificial stilling of the mind.

It is qualitatively different; in the abeyance of mental movement, the unconditioned energy of universal intelligence is released.

This intelligence is the moving sensitivity of the whole being.

With this movement of intelligence, awareness of the oneness of life blossoms and in every encounter in daily living, there is sensitivity to the sacredness, the divinity of living.

SILENCE

In sensitivity, you go back to your daily relationships innocently, tenderly, meeting the pain, the harshness of life, as you meet the beauty, the affection, and warmth of friendship.

When there is pain, there are tears; when there is pleasure, there are smiles, but these are flickering moments, like the dance of light rays on a leaf, which cannot be captured.

SILENCE

In sensitivity, you understand the movements of other people, you listen to them alertly, you look at them fully.

The perception is rich.

Your spontaneous response is richer than all the calculated reactions of the brain.

You speak without disturbing silence.

You move without peace being broken, shattered.

Movement becomes an extension of peace, and speech becomes an extension of silence.

SILENCE

Faith is the flower that blossoms in the heart when you are in direct, personal, immediate contact with the actuality of life, when there is nothing between life and you, no thought structure, no person, no theory.

It is communion between life and you.

Faith cannot be faith in a person, in ideas, but only faith in relation to the totality of living.

SILENCE

Faith is not fatalism, which is blind acceptance.
Faith receives what life brings, recognizing that
whatever life presents is significant.

SILENCE

Faith results in surrender, which is availability to life, to meet life as it comes in defenseless innocence.

Surrender is born of the awareness that there can be no separation from life and all its grandeur.

MEDITATION

Those who transcend the duality of silence and sound find themselves in the state of meditation.

Meditation is a state where there is no motion whatsoever, not even the movement of awareness or intelligence, not even the awareness that you are one with the universe or one with the totality.

In meditation you are at the "isness" of your being.

MEDITATION

Meditation is a total revolution in the perspective of life, in the way of living; it's an entirely new way of living from the wholeness of one's being.

One who lives in meditation meets each event of living as an expression of love of the divine.

MEDITATION

Meditation is an emptiness that contains all the creative powers within it.

It is like a drum.

The drum is empty but resonates and gives a tone to whoever touches it.

So a person in the state of nothingness responds in totality to every touch of a challenge, every encounter.

MEDITATION

Living in wholeness, the healing force contained in a person gets released.

The wholeness heals.

It's not a miracle; it's a happening in the dimension of totality, in the dimension of love.

MEDITATION

Living in the dimension of silence, awareness, and understanding does not remove us from the challenges of living.

We need to remind ourselves that the only divinity you and I will ever meet awaits us in the dawn, the beauty of the dawn, the sunrise that brings the mist, fog, cool breeze, the morning light dancing on the leaves of trees, making jewels of dewdrops on unfolding blossoms.

If these events are looked upon as mundane, if looking at them does not give the joy of being with the eternity of life, where are we going to find eternity?

Divinity comes to life in spontaneous communion with every event that the dawn brings to our doorstep.

MEDITATION

To live is to be vulnerable, receptive to the cosmic life around us.

To be free is to be vulnerable to the totality of which we are a part, without creating safe harbors for avoiding the joys and sorrows of living spontaneously, fully.

MEDITATION

It requires innocence and humility to let life operate on us.

Those who have the innocence and simplicity of humility find that they get cooperation from life, from life universal.

When they move in innocence and humility, the law of love cooperates with them, and such human beings find that they are helped from unexpected quarters.

As there is a law of gravity, there is a law of love.

MEDITATION

The timelessness of silence, the egolessness of love and compassion are the roots of our life.

Living on the mental level, drifting with the wind, the breeze, we are uprooted.

But in the magnificent emptiness of silence, in the communion with divinity, we are back at the roots of life, at the source of life.

Being at the source of life is being free.

MEDITATION

Only human beings living in freedom can create a new society, a new dimension of consciousness in which the tenderness of love and compassion can flower in each human heart.

Will you open with me
    invisible gates of a free
    world
Where mind limits not
    nor memory binds us?
Will you come with me
    to the land of eternity
Which lies beyond all frontiers
    which lies beyond life and
    death?
        —Vimala Thakar